Krishna, Buddha and Lao Tzu have a coffee with you

Jana Capri lives in Barcelona, Spain, speaks five languages and holds a degree in Translation and Interpretation from Charles University in Prague. She is a Master Practitioner in NLP (Neuro-Linguistic Programming) and has studied psychological astrology and creative writing. Jana is also a blogger and co-author of several books.

She has a strong interest in psychosomatics and personal growth and enjoys reading and writing books that inspire self-improvement and help others feel better about themselves.

Charan Díaz Arquillo is a psychologist based in Barcelona, Spain, with over twenty years of experience in psychotherapy, personal growth, educational psychology and organisational psychology. He holds a master's degree in Humanistic and Integrative Psychotherapy, as well as certifications in Mindfulness and Clinical Hypnosis from the University of Barcelona. Charan is also an author and co-author of several books.

He is passionate about Hindu and Greek philosophy, as well as oriental tales and mythology.

JANA CAPRI AND CHARAN DÍAZ

Krishna, Buddha and Lao Tzu have a coffee with you

ANSWERS TO LIFE'S DIFFICULT QUESTIONS

Published by Westland Books, a division of Nasadiya Technologies Private Limited, in 2025

No. 269/2B, First Floor, 'Irai Arul', Vimalraj Street, Nethaji Nagar, Alapakkam Main Road, Maduravoyal, Chennai 600095

Westland and the Westland logo are the trademarks of Nasadiya Technologies Private Limited, or its affiliates.

This English edition for the Indian Subcontinent published by arrangement with Suasive Consultants Private Limited (www.montsecortazar.com).

ISBN: 9789371975650

10 9 8 7 6 5 4 3

Illustration: Adobe Stock

Typeset by Jojy Philip

Printed at Thomson Press India Private Limited

All the religions of the world teach the same basic Truth. They all point to the same path. They all give the same message. They all reveal the same reality.

—Maharaj Charan Singh

CONTENTS

INTRODUCTION

The candidate, clad in his suit and tie, felt prepared to face any and all questions at this important job interview. He was an experienced professional in his field and was eager to show off his expert knowledge. But the interviewer's query threw him off balance; he had never been asked such a question before:

If you could pick one historical figure to have coffee with, who would you choose, and why?

Has it thrown you for a loop too? If such an encounter were possible, who would *you* choose to have coffee with? What questions would you ask them? How would they inspire you to live better? What would you learn from them?

Well, in this book, you will have the opportunity to have coffee with three of the wisest people in human history—Krishna, Buddha and Lao Tzu.

Throughout this read, we will enjoy imaginary coffee and see how these sages respond to questions about some persistent concerns in our lives, such as self-esteem issues, anxiety, depression, human relations, etc.

In addition, we will be in the company of psychology, to deepen our understanding of these important messages and their healthy positive influence. For this reason, we have chosen a psychologist to be our interviewer, to accompany us and put this ancient wisdom into a simpler, more contemporary context.

We will now comment on why these three characters have inspired us to create this imaginary coffee-meet:

KRISHNA

Why is it worth having coffee with Krishna?
In the jewel of Indian literature, the Bhagavad Gita, we find the character Krishna advising the warrior Arjuna. The hero is grief-stricken at having to face an enormous war that will pit him against many people, including his loved ones, but Krishna's company and wisdom lift his spirits and lead to his subsequent victory.

In addition to being a key character in the Gita, several pieces of archaeological and geographical evidence indicate the possible existence of Krishna about 5,000 years ago.

Krishna, with his cheerful and optimistic spirit, teaches us that the world we see is illusory, changing and ephemeral, and depends largely on our perception. He gives us important lessons about what really matters in life and reminds us that divinity is present in all of creation and, hence, the potential for wisdom and unconditional love exists within every human being.

Some of Krishna's key teachings include:

- How not to lose our fighting spirit
- Why we should do our duty regardless of life's ups and downs
- How to face our fears

- How not to lose heart when life throws challenges our way
- How to have unshakable faith.

BUDDHA

Why is it worth having coffee with Buddha?

Buddha's personal story is almost as extraordinary as his wisdom. Gautama Buddha was born a noble prince in a family of great prestige and power. But when he realised that human suffering transcends both wealth and poverty, he abandoned his noble and comfortable life to dedicate himself exclusively to spirituality. He practised spiritual meditation with discipline and determination for many years, seeking the inner answer to what truly frees us from suffering.

Buddha's life is an example of renunciation and detachment in exchange for achieving something greater: the avoidance of suffering due to unfulfilled desires, the attainment of inner freedom and the transcendence beyond the slavery entailed in a life lived only for selfish pleasures.

Buddha invites us to understand that life is much more than what we see on the outside. We have an opportunity to become consciously enlightened, to free ourselves from the limitations of our mind and to perceive the authentic reality, making the attainment of lasting inner happiness a certainty.

Some of Buddha's key teachings include:

- How to be freer
- How to achieve genuine happiness

- Understanding who we are and how our attention works
- How to stop suffering over the unavoidable things in life such as illness, old age and death
- Why it is important not to become so attached to material riches or the superficial pleasures of life.

LAO TZU

Why is it worth having coffee with Lao Tzu?
Little is known about Lao Tzu's life. Various sources indicate that he was a librarian at the imperial court of the Zhou dynasty in ancient China in the sixth century BCE, who later emigrated through the western borders of the country. What we do know is that his work *Tao Te Ching* has significantly influenced Chinese philosophy and became the basis of Taoism.

Lao Tzu speaks of the importance of being flexible and able to adapt to life's circumstances and our destiny. We must accept what is happening in life without clinging to it, just as it occurs in nature.

His teachings are strongly anchored in the Tao, which represents the eternal wisdom—that which is the source of all creation and is also found in ourselves. According to Lao Tzu, we must learn to tune in to the Tao so that we can make the most of our existence and be aligned with the purpose of our life.

Some of Lao Tzu's key teaching include:

- Mental flexibility

- How to adapt to the challenges of destiny
- How not to force things and let life flow
- How to master oneself
- How to live in balance with oneself and others, in tune with the Tao.

THE ROLE OF PSYCHOLOGY

The spiritual antidotes that we will find in this book correspond to questions about life. The psychologist plays the role of the interviewer, moderating this conversation with the aid of the practical viewpoint provided by psychology.

Part of our effort involved adapting the messages of the protagonists into a more modern and everyday language. We have paraphrased passages from the *Dhammapada* (Buddha), Bhagavad Gita (Krishna) and *Tao Te Ching* (Lao Tzu) for easy understanding and to give them a contemporary feel. We have shared the references to the quotations towards the end of the book.

In addition, at the end of each chapter, we share a psychological reflection and questions for the reader to contemplate. We believe that the answers Krishna, Buddha and Lao Tzu share offer psychologically interesting guidelines for our lives, which can positively influence the way we think, feel, speak and act.

* * *

As an aside, what character did the candidate in the suit and tie we talked about at the beginning of this introduction choose in the end? As it turns out, his answer was one of the three wise men in this book.

What about you—which character would you choose to go for a coffee with?

Hopefully, the answers from Buddha, Krishna and Lao Tzu will give you a good dose of inspiration. Even if just one word, idea or reflection adds a little encouragement, or proves to be a constructive influence in your life, as authors, we will consider that this work has been worthwhile.

We, for our part, have decided that we will continue to have relaxing teas and coffees with these wise men, letting their valuable, invisible company nurture our souls.

SOCIAL LIFE

Try to be yourself, without comparing or competing with others,
and others will respect you.

—Lao Tzu

Sitting cross-legged on the floor of a room are four people with very diverse appearances and attire, but who have one thing in common: they are meeting today to speak about life, the mind and human nature.

We see a man with long hair and a moustache, dressed in a traditional Chinese costume, with a slight smile on his face. Another person, wearing an earthy-toned robe, has a straight back and a fixed gaze. A third wears a crown with a peacock feather on his head, and you can see his bright eyes and an almost mischievous smile. The fourth and final person, clad in modern Western clothes, is trying to figure out how to position his legs so that he can sit comfortably, hoping they won't fall asleep during this interview. The four of them form a circle, each person with a cup of coffee before them.

As soon as the last man, the psychologist, begins to speak, the others look at him and listen without interrupting.

Psychologist: *Thank you very much for making this meeting possible. It is an honour to talk to you all. I hope we have a very meaningful dialogue today, where you shed light on important issues that affect us in our daily lives.*

To begin with, we will discuss how to live well in our society without giving undue importance to how other people see or treat us.

People are very affected when their loved ones or friends criticise them. What advice do you have for coping better with criticism?

Buddha: There is a proverb that goes, 'They criticise a person for being silent, they criticise a person for talking too much, and they criticise a person who does not talk enough.' As you can see, criticism is inevitable in this life.

Lao Tzu: That's true. My advice would be: don't take the opinions and prejudices of others too seriously. Once you manage to do that, you will no longer have any worries. For those who speak do not know, and those who really know do not speak.

Krishna: Do whatever you think is right. Not standing up for a good and just motive is akin to avoiding your responsibilities. Not only would you be going against your conscience, you will also end up being criticised and held in contempt by others for being too afraid.

DON'T STOP FIGHTING FOR WHAT IS RIGHT, REGARDLESS OF CRITICISM

Psychologist: *I understand. So, it is important to do what we consider right, regardless of what others think, because there will always be someone who criticises us, right?*

Buddha: Yes, it is important not to be influenced by the criticism of others. The day will come when those who now practise self-control and inner meditation will be envied by those who led a superficial life.

Krishna: Let us not forget that people who live only for merry-making and indulging in worldly pleasures do not make the most of their existence. But people who find satisfaction within themselves will live a more peaceful and superior life.

Lao Tzu: Even though you might consider yourself very strong when you control others, you can be truly powerful only when you have command over yourself.

MASTER YOURSELF AND FORGET THE REST

***Psychologist**: Many people tend to compare themselves with others, and this trait often affects their self-esteem. What advice do you have for them?*

Buddha: When a person appreciates what he has, even if it is very little, his life improves and he earns the respect of the gods.

Lao Tzu: Yes, we must learn to appreciate the gifts we receive from nature. It is only when you are content with what you have that you are truly rich.

Krishna: The wise person is always content with what God has given him. He is beyond the dualities of good and bad, no longer suffers from envy, and maintains inner stability both in times of success and failure.

APPRECIATE WHAT LIFE HAS GIVEN YOU AND AVOID COMPARING YOURSELF TO OTHERS

Psychologist: *I understand that in order to stop comparing ourselves to others and maintain a good rapport with the people around us, it is important that we are grateful for what life gives us. What other tips do you have for maintaining good communication and relationships with others?*

Krishna: When you engage with the right people from the heart, at the right time, in the right place and without expectations, you achieve balance in your life.

Lao Tzu: When you engage with others, it is important to be kind—to be a good person. Just be yourself and refrain from competing with others; in doing so, you will gain their respect.

Buddha: I agree. And regarding communication, I would add that it is better to share a single word that brings peace than to say a thousand useless words.

CHOOSE A GOOD TIME TO TALK, AND RELATE TO OTHERS FROM YOUR HEART, WITH KINDNESS

Psychologist: *Conflict between people is sometimes inevitable, and as often as we see what others do wrong, it is difficult for us to see the mistakes that we ourselves commit ...*

Buddha: You are correct, and that is why it's better not to think about what others do wrong and, instead, focus on your own transgressions and how you can do better.

Lao Tzu: It is wise to know what others are like, but first, you need to know yourself.

Krishna: Yes, and additionally, it is important to be kind to others—for their sake and also our own. Because when a person lives a life filled with love and appreciation towards their surroundings and desires happiness for all beings, they achieve self-fulfilment.

BEFORE ANALYSING OTHERS, FOCUS ON AND KNOW YOURSELF

***Psychologist**: In therapy, we see many cases where people suffer at work. It seems difficult to have a good relationship with superiors who abuse their power, and with colleagues who are constantly stressed. What should a person do in order not to lose his peace of mind at work?*

Krishna: The best thing to do is focus on what you yourself can do to fulfil your duty, no matter how humble it may seem. If you focus on what is up to you and accept your destiny, you will achieve harmony and inner peace.

Lao Tzu: Try to be yourself without comparing or competing with others, and you will gain the respect of those around you. Protect your inner peace by keeping in mind that a person without values will ask you to fulfil their desires, but a person with values will only ask you to do your own duty.

Buddha: In any case, we come back to the same point: focus on what you do and on what depends on you. Because if your mind is always disturbed by what others give you or don't give you, how do you expect to achieve inner freedom and enlightenment?

BE YOURSELF, DO YOUR DUTY AND DON'T HAVE TOO MANY EXPECTATIONS OF OTHERS

Guidance from Krishna, Buddha and Lao Tzu

1#

*Don't stop fighting for what is right,
regardless of criticism*

2#

Master yourself and forget the rest

3#

*Appreciate what life has given you and avoid
comparing yourself to others*

4#

*Choose a good time to talk, and relate to others from
your heart, with kindness*

5#

*Before analysing others, focus on
and know yourself*

6#

*Be yourself, do your duty and don't have too many
expectations of others*

The Psychologist Reflects

There is nothing that can brighten or darken our day as much as our interactions with other people. We are highly social beings and very sensitive when it pertains to getting along with other people. There is a lot of research that confirms that having quality relationships improves our well-being, makes us happier and is even good for our physical health.

But why is it so difficult to relate to other people? Whether in the family, with a partner, or at work, conflicts are inevitable. We can't *always* be fine with *everyone.* The question is how to maintain our mental and emotional equilibrium and learn to make the best of the circumstances, despite the misunderstandings and frictions that sometimes arise.

Introspection

The sages have spoken to us about various topics in this chapter, which we have summarised above.

But to better integrate this wisdom into our daily lives, to be able to remain calm and gain goodwill in our relationships with others, we can also ask ourselves the following questions that correspond to each guideline:

1. **Doing the right thing:** *Am I acting in a way that is consistent with my principles and values? Am I being negatively influenced by someone to the point of going against my principles? Do I need to assert myself more? In which situations and in what way?*

____

____

____

____

____

____

____

____

____

____

____

____

____

____

____

2. Practising self-control: *In which areas of my life, in which situations or with which person do I lack self-control? How can I gain more discipline? What can I do to become more aware of the way I act?*

3. Being grateful: *Am I grateful for the good things I have in my life? How can I focus more on what I have instead of what I lack? Can I be thankful for five things in my life right now?*

4. Being kind and doing things at the right moment: *Am I being kind to the people around me? How can I improve this? Am I speaking and acting at the right time, or do I lack tact when it comes to choosing the right moment? How can I be better at this?*

5. Self-focus: *How can I focus more on my life and not give too much importance to the opinions of others? If I were able to do so, what benefits would this have for me?*

6. Being less demanding of others: *Do I need to adjust my expectations of others? In what situations and with whom am I being too demanding lately? How does it make me feel, and how can I handle this better?*

My Notes:

WORK

Whatever you do, do it while maintaining your inner peace, and avoid taking decisions based on your ego. Don't let successes and failures throw you off balance.

—Krishna

Psychologist: *We have previously discussed the right attitude for the workplace. Continuing on this topic, we see that nowadays we tend to overload ourselves, often multitasking as we try to systematically get more and more done. What do the sages think about this?*

Krishna: There is a time to eat and a time to rest, a time to sleep and a time to be awake. Find balance in everything you do; this is the path that leads to calmness and helps avoid suffering.

Lao Tzu: If you pour too much into a vessel, it will eventually overflow; and if you sharpen a sword too much, it will wear out and last only a short while. The wise person chooses to withdraw in time.

Buddha: I agree that we must maintain a certain balance. An ignorant person always eats and sleeps too much, is overly enchanted with the material life and acts like a pig that prefers to wallow in the mud. A life without balance leads to a diminished existence.

FIND BALANCE IN WHAT YOU DO AND AVOID EXTREMES TO PREVENT SUFFERING

Psychologist: *On a psychological level, it is very important to find a balance between work, pleasure and rest, to prevent anxiety, depression or even physical illnesses resulting from chronic stress. But many people believe that working more will make them more successful, and that this will lead to happiness. Could you offer some wisdom on this lifestyle and people's approach to work in the pursuit of satisfaction?*

Buddha: There is no amount of gold in the world that can satisfy us, owing to the anxious and insatiable nature of our mind's desires. You will not find true satisfaction until you can let go of your wants and expectations, transcending them somehow.

Lao Tzu: When you empty your mind of expectations, desires and ambitions, it is easier to feel good about yourself. Because in the absence of desire, everything is peaceful.

Krishna: It is possible to fulfil your duties without losing sight of your soul. A person who enjoys his spirituality and attends to his soul, finds the true source of lasting peace. Such a person fulfils his duty with a higher, enlightened attitude.

EMPTY YOUR MIND OF DESIRES AND EXPECTATIONS, AND REMEMBER THAT MATERIAL WEALTH WILL NOT SATISFY YOU

Psychologist: *Many people desire to attain success at a professional level. However, is it possible to strive for success and riches, and at the same time maintain inner peace?*

Buddha: There is a difference between following the path of material wealth and pursuing inner wealth. My disciples will always hold that it is better to seek and gain freedom before pursuing a good reputation.

Lao Tzu: As Buddha says, there are two kinds of wealth in the world; which kind, then, should we seek?

What kind of person is so rich that they can always continue to give without exhausting their supply? The person who has discovered the peace of the Tao within! This inner peace is a source that never runs dry. In contrast, material success is like standing with one foot on a higher step than the other—it is an unstable posture that can change at any moment. Put both your feet on solid ground, and it will be easier to maintain balance.

Krishna: In any case, whatever you do, carry it out while maintaining your inner peace, and avoid making decisions driven by your ego. Let neither success nor failure throw you off balance.

REFLECT ON THE TYPE OF WEALTH YOU ARE LOOKING FOR, BECAUSE ONLY ONE WILL BRING YOU INNER PEACE

***Psychologist**: At work, we sometimes face ethical conflicts where we do not know the right course of action—for instance, when asked to do things that might harm someone. However, since our job is our main source of income, how can we make the right choice when confronted with such situations?*

Buddha: It's normal to feel confused as, to the ignorant, harmful actions may seem sweet at first—only for them to have to swallow the bitter fruits of their actions later and face the pain that follows. But we know that an action is right when, at the end of the day, we feel no regret, our conscience is clear and we enjoy the sweet rewards (good consequences) of our efforts.

Lao Tzu: That's right. Always do the right thing, because even if you think you have reasonable motives, acting wrongly will bring consequences in the end.

Krishna: Additionally, thinking in the right way is as important as acting with integrity. If you stop yourself from doing wrong but still harbour the desire to do them, you are deceiving yourself with this contradiction. You will find it impossible to gain peace.

THINK AND ACT IN SUCH A WAY THAT YOU CAN ALWAYS KEEP YOUR CONSCIENCE CLEAR AND NOT REGRET IT LATER

Psychologist: *Fulfilling worldly duties and maintaining even a degree of inner calm seem like incompatible concepts. How, then, can we achieve both in this life?*

Krishna: If you fail to do your duty you will not be free. It is inevitable that some kind of action must be taken to fulfil certain duties; this is nature's law. The point is to act with a transcendental attitude—that is, not neglect your spiritual side.

Buddha: If a person acts in accordance to their own values when fulfilling their duties, they are already on the right path.

Lao Tzu: I would add that excellence consists of letting things flow and adapting flexibly to everything that comes your way. When you don't resist so much with your mind, you will come to understand that the Tao expresses itself in all that happens in the world.

DON'T AVOID YOUR RESPONSIBILITIES, SIMPLY ACT WITH VALUES AND LET THINGS HAPPEN

Psychologist: *Work is necessary, but it generates a lot of stress and anxiety in our society today. What final advice can you offer for maintaining a more serene attitude towards work?*

Krishna: Do what you have to do, but avoid focusing only on material rewards, as this can lead to attachment to your work. Remember that the spiritual goal is superior to work.

Lao Tzu: The ignorant person values only the material wealth he gets from others. Work as a wise person would—without any expectations of worldly benefits.

Buddha: My advice would be: always act with good intentions, and you will be filled with joy. To achieve inner contentment is the greatest treasure.

DO THE BEST YOU CAN WITHOUT EXPECTATIONS, AND TRY TO LOOK BEYOND THE MATERIAL REWARDS

Guidance from Krishna, Buddha and Lao Tzu

1#

Find balance in what you do and avoid extremes to prevent suffering

2#

Empty your mind of desires and expectations, and remember that material wealth will not satisfy you

3#

Reflect on the type of wealth you are looking for, because only one will bring you inner peace

4#

Think and act in such a way that you can always keep your conscience clear and not regret it later

5#

Don't avoid your responsibilities, simply act with values and let things happen

6#

Do the best you can without expectations, and try to look beyond the material rewards

The Psychologist Reflects

Today, we are experiencing more stress than ever in our professional lives. Statistics from Western countries state that one in two workers experiences excessive levels of stress at work, causing them to suffer every day.

Work is no longer what it should be—a source of income that allows us to eat three square meals a day, keep a roof over our heads and maintain our health.

These days we are also concerned about status (is my job respected in society?), stability (stable company, fixed contract?), relationships with others (my workmate is no longer speaking to me; have I done something wrong?), the future (where will this job take me in five years?), work-life balance (how will I manage to fulfil my work responsibilities while ensuring I spend time with my family?) and so on and so forth.

Work-related stress is one of the most frequent issues encountered in psychotherapy. How can we be better off?

Introspection

We can ask ourselves some questions to find out how we are handling this subject. The questions are directly related to the advice the sages have given us in this chapter:

1. **Maintaining balance:** *At this point in my life, do I work to live or live to work? How do I strike a better balance between work and free time? What concrete actions can I take to achieve this?*

2. Reviewing your objectives: *What am I looking for in life? What is my goal? Does this goal bring me closer to my inner peace, or does it pull me further away?*

3. Managing expectations better: *How can I be less demanding and critical of myself and others, and develop more calm and confidence? What level of material success do I expect to achieve? How are my ambitions affecting or impairing my well-being?*

4. Making conscious decisions: *When we have to make a decision, we ask ourselves: if I do this, will I have a clear conscience? Do I have any pending decisions to make that weigh on my mind? What would a person I admire for their values decide if they were in my place?*

5. Reviewing what is in our power and what is not: *Do I clearly understand what is in my hands (my responsibility) and what I must leave in the hands of others or destiny? In which situations do I find it hardest to distinguish this? How can I improve in this respect?*

6. Maintaining a positive attitude: *How can I maintain a more positive attitude towards work? What specific things could I focus on to be a little more at ease when it comes to my profession?*

My Notes:

DEPRESSION

We should not expect only moments of happiness, nor get too caught up in sadness. We had better learn to keep our balance beyond the ups and downs of life.

—Krishna

Psychologist: *How can we be happier with our life? Experiencing fulfilment in life seems to be a complicated issue for many people.*

Lao Tzu: When you accept that things are the way they are and learn to be content with what life has given you, you will realise that you want for nothing and that the whole world belongs to you. But if you believe that you lack certain possessions to be happy, or if your happiness depends on others, you will never truly find joy.

Krishna: I agree with Lao Tzu and would add only that the spiritual person does not depend too much on the external world, as they find contentment from within.

Buddha: Of course, to find inner happiness is the greatest treasure.

TAKE CARE OF YOUR INNER HAPPINESS AND UNDERSTAND THAT THE WORLD OUTSIDE CANNOT GIVE YOU ANYTHING VALUABLE

Psychologist: *And how can we live better with the losses that life confronts us with? You can't always win—sometimes you win and sometimes you lose, right?*

Buddha: Most people enjoy pleasure but find themselves incapable of coping with the loss of it; they end up suffering for the lack of it. That is why the person who manages to go beyond pleasure and pain is freer, because they cease to depend on the chains that bind most people, and thus 'wins' even when they lose.

Krishna: It is best to face the struggles of life by cultivating inner peace. If you manage to maintain peace in your soul in times of pleasure and in times of pain, when you win as well as when you lose, when you succeed and when you fail, that inner peace will ensure that you are prepared to face anything.

Lao Tzu: What more can I add? No matter how much you cling to things, one day you will inevitably lose them. The wise person is not attached to his possessions or ideas, and lets things in life take their course.

TRY TO ACHIEVE A STATE OF MIND WHERE WINNING AND LOSING DO NOT AFFECT YOU

Psychologist: *Going by what you are saying, it is essential not to give too much importance to success and worldly events so that we do not get emotionally destabilised. But for many people, what happens in their lives is so real and felt so intensely that it is difficult for them to maintain a sense of detachment. What would you tell people who feel this way?*

Buddha: When a person recognises that this world is as illusory as a mirage and as short-lived as a foam bubble, they will stop suffering for unreal things.

Krishna: The external world is ever-changing, temporary and will always be deceptive and unreal. But there is a deeper truth—unchanging and eternal—that lies beyond appearances. A wise person recognises and lives with this understanding.

Lao Tzu: Once we realise that everything in this world is constantly changing, we will see that there is no point in holding on to it. Therefore, wanting to control the future is absurd.

THIS WORLD IS ILLUSORY; TO ALLEVIATE SUFFERING, FOCUS ON SEEKING OUT THE TRUTH

Psychologist: *If the material world is illusory and real happiness is within us, does that mean nothing can truly harm us?*

Buddha: Well, look—if your thoughts lead you in the wrong direction, they can cause greater harm than an enemy might inflict on another.

Krishna: Of course, we have to be careful, for there are three gates that lead to hell and the loss of one's soul: the gate of lust, the gate of anger and the gate of greed. It is best to avoid these three gates if you do not wish harm upon yourself.

Lao Tzu: Human beings and their ways of living reminds me of a carpenter. A carpenter is fortunate if he or she doesn't injure their own hand while working with wood. Similarly, one is lucky when one manages to not hurt oneself.

CONTROL YOUR THOUGHTS AND AVOID LUST, ANGER AND GREED, LEST YOU HARM YOURSELF

Psychologist: *According to your point of view, how does faith relate to our well-being?*

Lao Tzu: Faith is of vital importance. When you focus your attention on the Tao, the sky shines and the earth is fertile and stable; everything flourishes, everything fits and all beings are transformed and are content to be what they are. There is balance. But when you become distracted and distant from the Tao, the sky seems dark, the earth is barren and unstable, nothing fits, and all beings—and in general, everything—seem to lose their balance.

Krishna: When you have faith, you have wisdom. With wisdom providing balance and faith at the centre of your life, you attain absolute serenity. But without faith and wisdom, your soul is filled with doubts and you are lost. For neither this present world, nor the future, nor existential fulfilment can be enjoyed by those without faith who live full of doubts.

Buddha: If your thinking is irrational, you will not know which path will lead you to see reality. And if your faith is full of doubts, you will never experience inner fulfilment. But one who takes care of their own thoughts and has overcome the anxiety produced by expectations and desires, who has transcended labels, becomes enlightened and no longer suffers from fear.

TAKE CARE OF YOUR FAITH AND YOU WILL BECOME A WISER AND MORE SERENE PERSON

Psychologist: *Going by what you say, there is no doubt that people who pay attention to spirituality are more satisfied and at peace. Can you speak a little more about the importance of caring for the soul?*

Lao Tzu: When someone focuses their attention on the Tao, they transform and evolve gradually in a natural manner. They are content with the simplicity of daily life, experience inner harmony, and desire few things. And by no longer depending on their desires and expectations, they achieve inner peace.

Buddha: Whoever lives consciously at all times knows and evaluates himself constantly, and strives sincerely to attain nirvana, will cease to suffer from vices and human passions.

Krishna: That's right, let us not forget that our soul is a lamp that is lit permanently, never shaken or extinguished because it can withstand any wind. What is more important, then, than the soul?

THE BEST WAY TO ACHIEVE PEACE OF MIND IS TO TAKE CARE OF YOUR SOUL

Psychologist: *What advice do you have for coping better with the ups and downs of life, and the fear of the future?*

Lao Tzu: Everything changes, so why hold on to anything? If you try to control your future, you will most likely hurt yourself. Try to be flexible.

Krishna: We should not expect only moments of happiness, nor get too caught up in sadness. We should learn to keep our balance beyond the ups and downs of life.

Buddha: This body sometimes suffers and sometimes is well; it's always changing and never permanent, isn't it? The body ages, material possessions perish, but virtue and wisdom remain unaffected by time. Remember this to keep calm.

SOMETIMES WE ARE ALL RIGHT, SOMETIMES WE ARE NOT, BUT REMEMBER THAT WISDOM DOES NOT CHANGE OVER TIME

Psychologist: *The fear of death seems to be one of the greatest fears that anyone can experience. How can we change our perspective about death to feel more at peace about it?*

Buddha: As I have already said, when you realise that this world is as resilient as a foam bubble, you will no longer fear death. I have seen the builder—the creator of this house we call life, and I have been able to free myself from this samsara. You can achieve the same.

Lao Tzu: The person who has achieved the Tao knows that death is inevitable and that there is no point in clinging to anything. They do not live in any illusion and do not resist. Hence, they are better prepared to face death, like a person who is ready to go to sleep after a good day's work.

Krishna: Every being who is born in the material world has to die. But in every being, there is an immortal soul. So why be afraid of death?

WHEN YOU UNDERSTAND THE NATURE OF THE SOUL AND SEE THAT THIS WORLD IS ONLY AN ILLUSION, YOU WILL NO LONGER FEAR DEATH

Guidance from Krishna, Buddha and Lao Tzu

1#

Take care of your inner happiness and understand that the world outside cannot give you anything valuable

2#

Try to achieve a state of mind where winning and losing do not affect you

3#

This world is illusory; to alleviate suffering, focus on seeking out the truth

4#

Control your thoughts and avoid lust, anger and greed, lest you harm yourself

5#

Take care of your faith and you will become a wiser and more serene person

6#

The best way to achieve peace of mind is to take care of your soul

7#

Sometimes we are all right, sometimes we are not, but remember that wisdom does not change over time

8#

When you understand the nature of the soul and see that this world is only an illusion, you will no longer fear death

The Psychologist Reflects

Human beings have achieved great things in this world. Thanks to scientific and technological advancement, we have gained a level of comfort that our ancestors could never even have imagined.

However, are we happier than the previous generations?

Apparently not. When you observe children—some playing joyfully in the sand, others surrounded by the latest technology—you'll notice that their happiness isn't determined by what they possess. In many cases, the child with less is just as happy, if not more. This reminds us that mental well-being has less to do with material conditions and more to do with how we live our lives.

Introspection

Let's look at how we can transform the pearls of wisdom from Krishna, Buddha and Lao Tzu into questions for self-evaluation, and figure out how to apply the sages' advice to our lives:

1. Knowing where to look for happiness: *What is my definition of happiness? What does my happiness depend on? What things in my life, or goals I wish to achieve, provide me with false happiness that is not lasting? What can give me genuine and lasting happiness?*

2. Maintaining mental and emotional stability: *What situations, things or people in my life have power over my mental and emotional balance? How do they affect me? How can I get them to not matter so much to me—what should I do or think?*

3. Distinguishing the illusory (false) from the real (true): *Am I putting my happiness in the hands of the future (goals to achieve, plans and desires to fulfil that will make me 'happy')? Does my happiness depend on something that is not under my control? If so, how can I make my well-being depend only on me and not on factors outside myself?*

4. Being self-aware and maintaining self-control: *What makes me feel really good and what is giving me only fleeting pleasure? Am I doing things that are hurting me? Is there an area in my life where I need to gain self-control? What will improve in my life if I gain more restraint in that area?*

5. Having faith: *Do I have faith in God, Energy, Creative Intelligence, the Universe or some other entity greater than myself? If so, how does having faith benefit me? At what points in my life has having faith helped me? How can I get more life satisfaction from faith? If I don't have any faith, am I willing to explore how faith might help me gain calmness, gratitude and life satisfaction?*

6. Maintaining spiritual practice: *What am I currently doing to take care of my soul, my spirituality? What spiritual practice am I curious to try and how can I get started?*

7. Accepting ups and downs and focusing on what doesn't change: How would it help me to think that the problem I am going through is just one more small chapter in the great book of my life that contains thousands of chapters? Can I remember some bad phases in my life that I have already managed to overcome successfully? What attitude could I adopt to cope better with the ups and downs in my life?

8. Understanding the nature of life and death: *What is my concept of death? Do I believe in the immortality of the soul? In what ways could I be less afraid and more at peace with the subject of death? What advice from Krishna, Buddha or Lao Tzu on the subject of death most reassures me and how can I integrate it into my life?*

My Notes:

ANXIETY

If you allow the wind to blow you around in all directions, you will lose touch with your roots. In the same way, if you allow your mental restlessness to agitate you, you lose touch with your centre, with who you really are.

—Lao Tzu

Psychologist: *Today, there is a great deal of status anxiety. People tend to compare themselves to others in terms of position in life and possessions they have, and suffer due to their own ambitions. What wisdom can you share with me on this subject?*

Lao Tzu: Of course, the ambitious and capricious person is ruled by their desires and finds it very difficult to live serenely and with inner peace. If you don't expect anything, you will never be disappointed.

Krishna: On the other hand, a wise soul who has already attained a certain inner peace does not get too attached to things and, hence, does not expect too much from anyone or anything. And so, they are no longer stressed by the successes and failures that occur throughout life.

Buddha: If you practise some self-control, you can live calmly. If you manage to free yourself from the whims and desires of the mind, you will evolve inwardly to such an extent that you will never suffer fear, and you will awaken from the sleep of this materialistic world.

PRACTISE SELF-CONTROL AND DO NOT STRESS ABOUT THE MATERIALISTIC WORLD

***Psychologist**: Should we fight to change the world, even if it means coming into conflict with others?*

Lao Tzu: I believe that a noble person seeks peace and tranquillity—for that is what they value most—and only fights or takes up arms when it is unavoidable. Such a person does not wish other people ill or rejoice when they win against others.

Buddha: We are in this world to live in harmony and peace. A person who knows this does not fight against others.

Krishna: Such a fight should take place within yourself. You can be a warrior and conquer the powerful enemies of the soul—desire and expectations. Focus on the spiritual, which lies beyond logic, and there you will find inner peace.

SEEK TO BE IN HARMONY WITH OTHERS; TRUE WARRIORS FIGHT WITHIN THEMSELVES

Psychologist: *I understand that you place great value on harmony—both within ourselves and in our relationships with others. What more can you add on this topic?*

Buddha: A person who lives in harmony leads a more fortunate existence. It is important to live in harmony both with others and ourselves, and it will do one good to realise this sooner rather than later.

Krishna: No one can truly be wise without harmony. Because without harmony and balance, one cannot practise introspection. If you cannot observe your inner self, you cannot find peace, and without peace how can anyone be happy?

Lao Tzu: Certain qualities facilitate harmony. Even nature itself teaches us in various ways that to be alive means to be flexible. For example, human beings are soft and flexible at birth, but when we die, we are rigid. Plants are also tender and flexible initially but, with time, they dry up and become hard, brittle and easily broken. Being flexible and sensitive is always better than the opposite.

LIVE IN HARMONY WITH YOURSELF, AND
BE SENSITIVE AND FLEXIBLE

Psychologist: *In our mind we have too many negative thoughts during the day, which feed our anxiety, fear and anger. How does a wise person manage the flow of negative thoughts?*

Lao Tzu: That's true. To become calmer, we must cleanse our mind of unpleasant thoughts and free ourselves of our harmful vices.

Krishna: The key to achieving this, to calm our mind and gain inner peace is meditation.

Buddha: If a person speaks and acts with a mind full of negative thoughts, suffering will follow them—just as the wheels of a cart follow the animal that pulls it. But if a person speaks and acts with a mind full of good thoughts, inner peace will always follow, just as one's shadow follows one everywhere.

BE AT PEACE AND CLEAR YOUR MIND OF NEGATIVE THOUGHTS THROUGH MEDITATION

Psychologist: *Sometimes we feel as though our minds are overloaded, making it difficult for us to prioritise and focus. Would you like to comment on this issue?*

Lao Tzu: If you allow the wind to pull you in all directions, you lose touch with your roots. In the same way, if you allow your mental restlessness to agitate you, you lose contact with your centre, with who you really are.

Buddha: Continuing with the wind metaphor, just as the wind can shake a fragile tree, the ups and downs in life can shake people who live only for fun and pleasure. But a person with values, who finds harmony within themselves, is like a great rock—unalterable by the changing world around them.

Krishna: Your worst enemy is your own restless mind. If you gain mental self-control, the world will be a better and friendlier place for you.

IF YOU ALLOW YOUR MIND TO BE TROUBLED, YOU ARE LIVING WITH AN ENEMY AND MOVING AWAY FROM YOUR REAL SELF

Psychologist: *What should we do when we make a mistake involving something important in our lives?*

Lao Tzu: Before taking any action, reflect. Try to anticipate problems before they arise. Avoid acting in haste, as you might make a mistake.

Buddha: I agree with Lao Tzu. But once the mistake is made, the most important thing you can do is learn from it so that you never repeat it. Because if we repeat an action too many times, the mind can get used to it and may even find pleasure in destructive vices. When you repeat a vice, even a small one, it makes you a worse person; a glass is filled drop by drop.

Krishna: In any case, do not be discouraged. It is better to act than to do nothing. You need actions to fulfil your responsibilities in this life; this is the way life moves forward. If you think about it, even your own body would not function without the actions of life—the functioning of our organs—unfolding within you.

THINK AND THEN ACT, AND ONCE A MISTAKE HAS BEEN MADE, LEARN FROM IT SO AS NOT TO REPEAT IT

Guidance from Krishna, Buddha and Lao Tzu

1#

Practise self-control and do not stress about the materialistic world

2#

Seek to be in harmony with others; true warriors fight within themselves

3#

Live in harmony with yourself, and be sensitive and flexible

4#

Be at peace and clear your mind of negative thoughts through meditation

5#

If you allow your mind to be troubled, you are living with an enemy and moving away from your real self

6#

Think and then act, and once a mistake has been made, learn from it so as not to repeat it

The Psychologist Reflects

Our mind can be our best friend or our worst enemy. How many times have we suffered for imagining something terrible that ended up never happening? How many times have we made a big fuss over something unimportant? How many times have we regretted not having controlled our emotions?

One way to reduce depression and anxiety, and better our level of emotional well-being, is to train our mind to become our ally.

This is certainly not an easy task. It requires a lot of work on our part: self-awareness, self-control, willpower, determination, a willingness to learn from our mistakes, etc.

The wise remind us that it is certainly possible to live with less anxiety, and the power to do so is in our hands.

Introspection

Let's now look at the tips that have been shared in this chapter and the questions we can ask ourselves.

1. **Not being stressed about money**: *On a scale of 0 to 10, how much importance do I give to money and material things? How does this affect my mental well-being? What can I think or do to be more at peace with this issue?*

2. Not fighting with others: *Is there a person in my life who influences my well-being too much? How does he/she affect me? How can I make them affect me less? How can I focus more on myself and less on what others are doing?*

3. Being at peace with oneself, being sensitive and flexible: *On a scale of 0 to 10, how satisfied am I with myself at this particular time in my life? How can I be at peace with myself? How can sensitivity and flexibility help me better my relationships with myself and others?*

4. Monitoring negative thoughts: *Am I able to observe my thoughts and recognise which ones are currently dominating my mind? How do these thoughts affect me? Which thought can I adopt and repeat to myself today to help me feel better?*

5. Controlling your restless mind: *Am I aware of it when I am stressed and my mind won't stop? What exercise or technique can I learn to become calm during stressful times? What concrete benefit could I gain from becoming calmer?*

6. Thinking before acting and learning from mistakes: *Can I remember the last time it helped me to think before making an important decision? At times when I tend to be more impulsive, how can I make myself stop and think before I act? What was the last serious mistake I made and what have I learnt from that experience?*

My Notes:

ANGER MANAGEMENT

The person who controls his growing anger knows how to control his emotions, just as a good driver knows how to control his vehicle at full speed. But if he were not able to control his vehicle at high speed, could we call him a good driver?

—Buddha

Psychologist: *Many people come to therapy with the objective of learning how to manage their anger and negative reactions when things do not go as they expected. What do the sages say about anger management?*

Krishna: Of course, learning to control negative emotions is extremely important. Because an excess of passion leads to a disturbed mind, and a disturbed mind becomes scattered, forgets what is important, and does not do its duty. Avoiding your duties leads to confusion and poor decision-making—it brings about a breakdown in clarity and purpose, and clouds your judgement—and an irrational mind leads people to destroy themselves.

Buddha: As Krishna says, anger has consequences. The person who controls his growing anger knows how to control his emotions, just as a good driver knows how to control their vehicle even at full speed. But if they were not able to control the vehicle, could we call them a good driver?

Lao Tzu: We need to purify our inner self so that our energy and mentality are as pure as that of a newborn baby.

MANAGING YOUR ANGER IS LIKE MANAGING A SPEEDING CAR; IT'S WORTH DOING

Psychologist: *Can you comment more on how anger affects us? According to a spiritual point of view, why is it better to avoid it?*

Krishna: Many times, it is our desires that make us angry. Your anxiety over whether your wishes will be fulfilled can lead to ill-temper, and this clouds your reason, just as smoke prevents you from seeing the fire, or dust covers the mirror. And as you can imagine, a cloudy mind does not aid us in developing our consciousness.

Buddha: As Krishna says, anger and ego cannot harm you when you do not desire anything, are not bound to anything and claim nothing as belonging to you.

Lao Tzu: In my opinion, the ordinary person never has enough and is therefore always striving to have more. Then, when they don't succeed, anger arises. However, a person attuned to the Tao never aspires to great things—and that is how they achieve them. Such a person accepts the difficulties of life and does not perceive them as problems.

IF YOU HAVE NO DESIRES, ANGER WILL HAVE NO EFFECT ON YOU

Psychologist: *The importance of self-control is clear, as it helps us avoid doing things that we may regret later. Some may think that anger is justified—for instance, if we are attacked and we strike back as a defence mechanism. What do you think of this?*

Buddha: You can never get rid of anger and attain inner peace if you keep thinking things like 'They insulted me', 'They hurt me', 'They manipulated me', 'They stole from me', etc. Because there is the universal fact that hatred is not extinguished by hatred; it can only be overcome by love.

Lao Tzu: That's right, love is a good antidote: to win, attack with love, and to defend yourself, armour yourself with love. You expect heaven to be compassionate to you, but in reality, it is heaven that expects you to be compassionate.

Krishna: It is important to keep in mind that anger and materialistic ambition come from the lowest nature of the human being. They are obstacles that keep you from inner peace.

THE BEST COUNTER-ATTACK AND THE BEST DEFENCE AGAINST SOCIAL SITUATIONS THAT DISTURB US IS LOVE

Psychologist: *I understand that we should not become angry or attack others; instead, we should exercise self-control and consider people with greater compassion and love. Any more advice for situations where other people get on our nerves and we find it hard to keep calm?*

Buddha: It is better not to ruminate about the bad things others have done to you or how you think they should behave. Instead, think about what you can learn from your mistakes and how you should act going forward.

Lao Tzu: Why get angry? The best way to be aligned with heaven and enjoy its harmony is to not be irritated or confrontational with each other.

Krishna: Getting angry is not really worth it, for anger is one of the gates that lead to hell and destruction. When a person seeks self-realisation, they avoid the darkness of anger and focus on what brings well-being to their soul.

DO NOT GET TOO ANGRY WITH OTHERS AND DO NOT HOLD GRUDGES

***Psychologist**: You have said that anger is an obstacle to self-realisation. Can you speak a little more about how anger negatively affects our spiritual development?*

Lao Tzu: From my point of view, anger is contrary to the harmony of the Tao. Because anger seeks to precipitate the evolution of things, indicates a general impatience towards the natural order in life and involves using too much energy, which can lead to exhaustion or destruction.

Krishna: When the mind loses harmony and balance, it can no longer appreciate the spiritual part of existence. But when a person achieves inner harmony, and if they are wise and make a sincere effort, they can enjoy the full experience of life. So, until one can control one's anger and passions, one cannot see the light in this life.

Buddha: If you learn to control your angry thoughts, you will enjoy greater harmony and existential satisfaction. Also, only those who do no harm to anyone and who maintain good self-control can attain nirvana.

CONTROLLING ANGER AND PASSIONS, AND NOT HURTING ANYONE, IS A GOOD FIRST STEP ON THE PATH TO INNER PEACE

Psychologist: *It has become clear that controlling our negative emotions is important for our well-being and spiritual development. But how can one manage not to be carried away by toxic emotions?*

Buddha: Remain conscious day and night, search within yourself and dedicate all your energy to achieving nirvana. Then your mind is automatically freed from passions such as anger.

Lao Tzu: If you want to manage anger, always remember that you hold these three treasures within yourself: compassion, moderation and humility. That way you can be courageous, generous and a good example to others.

Krishna: I would add that your mind becomes your own worst enemy when you do not seek happiness within yourself. But if you find your soul, your mind will become your best friend.

TURN YOUR MIND INTO YOUR FRIEND, BE A GOOD PERSON, AND YOU WILL BE FREE OF NEGATIVE EMOTIONS

Guidance from Krishna, Buddha and Lao Tzu

1#

Managing your anger is like managing a speeding car; it's worth doing

2#

If you have no desires, anger will have no effect on you

3#

The best counter-attack and the best defence against social situations that disturb us is love

4#

Do not get too angry with others and do not hold grudges

5#

Controlling anger and passions, and not hurting anyone, is a good first step on the path to inner peace

6#

Turn your mind into your friend, be a good person, and you will be free of negative emotions

The Psychologist Reflects

Anger, rage and fury seldom lead to a good outcome. Getting too upset prevents us from thinking clearly, and when we don't think clearly, we end up making more mistakes—we react impulsively, and we hurt both others and ourselves. No one wants to end up lonely, unhealthy and bitter, yet these are the consequences of failing to control one's own anger.

So, is it possible to live without letting ourselves be carried away by negative emotions? The sages tell us that we have to at least try. We have to realise the harmful consequences of anger and try to become more aware, learn to control ourselves, and rationalise.

We can always look for and use psychological resources to help us manage the mental, emotional, communicative and behavioural aspects of anger. It is an endeavour for our inner self that we must keep at throughout our lives.

Introspection

Based on the practical advice in this chapter, we can ask ourselves the following questions:

1. Managing anger: *When do I have the hardest time controlling my anger? The next time I feel angry, can I stop for a moment, take a breath and think about how I can react better? What have I already tried that didn't work and what can I still try to better control my negative emotions?*

2. Keeping an eye on desires: *The last time I got very angry about something was my reaction related to any unfulfilled expectations or desires? How do my desires influence my day-to-day life—do they move me closer to, or further away from a state of tranquillity? What would be different if I had more flexible expectations about the course of my life?*

3. Seeing problems from a perspective of love: *If I think of a current problem, how might I see the same issue—and myself—through the eyes of someone who loves me very much and wants the best for me? How would such an action change my perspective? If I have a conflict with someone, what difference would it make if I were to consider the other person with more regard and compassion? How do I feel when I try to see what is bothering me or causing me stress with an attitude of greater kindness, love or caring?*

4. Not getting angry and not holding a grudge: *On a scale of 0 to 10, how often and how intensely do I usually get angry in my daily life? And, on a scale of 0 to 10, do I usually hold a grudge when something unpleasant happens to me or someone I care for? What benefit would it bring me to be more understanding with others, to gain emotional self-control and to learn to ask for what I want in a more assertive way?*

5. Not hurting anyone: *When was the last time I hurt someone, either with my words or actions? How do I feel about it? In what situations and how often do I tend to hurt others, and how can I improve this situation?*

6. Being a good person: *What values are most important to me? In my opinion, what values does a good person follow in their life? If there is a difference, what is the reason for it?*

My Notes:

SELF-ESTEEM

The world accepts you easily when you accept yourself.

—Lao Tzu

Psychologist: *Many people are affected by what others say about them, and this can impact their self-esteem. I imagine that a wise person is indifferent to the compliments and criticisms of others …*

Buddha: To such a person, I would say: don't give so much importance to what others say or you will lose sight of what is really important in life. Rather, focus on your personal responsibilities, on how you respond to different situations in life, and on what actions you take and do not take.

Lao Tzu: The wise person believes in themselves and, therefore, does not try to convince others of their viewpoints. Having found inner contentment, they no longer wish for anyone's approval. The world accepts you easily when you accept yourself.

Krishna: Of course. And let us not forget that the wise person is content with and trusts in what God has given them.

FOCUS ON HOW YOU ACT, NOT ON OTHERS. ACCEPT YOURSELF AND LEAVE THE REST IN GOD'S HANDS

Psychologist: *When people do not achieve what they set out to do, or when their plans do not work out, it is easy for them to become discouraged. What would you say to such a person?*

Krishna: I would say: abandon your expectations and look beyond your ego. Leave your worries and the results of your actions in the hands of God. Navigate life's challenges while taking care of your inner peace.

Buddha: Plans? Worldly achievements? The greatest victory is the one you achieve within yourself—it is superior to defeating a thousand warriors.

Lao Tzu: Nothing more needs to be added. Let us remember that the Tao is within us and it is the greatest thing that any human being can achieve in this life.

THE GREATEST ACHIEVEMENT IN LIFE IS WINNING THE BATTLE WITHIN YOURSELF

Psychologist: *I understand that since the world is illusory and changing, there is really no point in fighting against it. Can you comment further on how to master oneself and, thus, achieve greater inner happiness?*

Buddha: The kings of the past might have looked mighty when they rode trained elephants. But the real mastery lies in training and educating yourself. This way, even if you are offended and criticised by others, you do not lose your inner peace.

Lao Tzu: I would put it to you in the following way: there is a space within you, beyond your thoughts, where the heart is filled with peace. If you discover your true origin, (your spiritual heart, the inner Tao), values like tolerance, simplicity, existential joy and affection—like a grandmother's love—will naturally appear within you. And in that moment, you will come to the self-realisation that you deserve respect befitting a king.

Krishna: Inner happiness? Willpower, faith, serenity, kindness and generosity—in short, a heart full of values is the true inner treasure of a divine soul.

FIND THE SACRED (SPIRITUAL) SPACE WITHIN YOURSELF; THE VALUES WORTHY OF A GOOD PERSON WILL NATURALLY APPEAR WITHIN YOU

Psychologist: *What do the sages say about taking care of our health, and how is it related to inner happiness?*

Krishna: It is as simple as this: the healthy person prefers healthy food—those foods that contribute to their physical and mental health, that give them strength and promote longevity. Foods that are pleasant, soothing and nourishing facilitate a happy heart.

Buddha: Taking care of your health is very important. Satisfaction is the best treasure, and confidence is your closest friend. But nirvana is superior to everything else.

Lao Tzu: The only thing that truly nourishes us is the inner Tao. When your life is centred on the Tao, you naturally take care of your health, and you no longer fear what you might encounter on life's path.

TAKING CARE OF YOUR HEALTH AND NUTRITION IS AN IMPORTANT BASIS FOR THE CARE OF YOUR INNER SELF

Guidance from Krishna, Buddha and Lao Tzu

1#

Focus on how you act, not on others. Accept yourself and leave the rest in God's hands

2#

The greatest achievement in life is winning the battle within yourself

3#

Find the sacred (spiritual) space within yourself; the values worthy of a good person will naturally appear within you

4#

Taking care of your health and nutrition is an important basis for the care of your inner self

The Psychologist Reflects

Taking care of our self-esteem is a topic that has gained a lot of traction in modern psychology. We want to learn how to feel better about ourselves, how to make others respect and treat us well, and how to be happier.

How do the ancient sages and mystics view the subject of self-esteem?

They tell us that yes, we have to take care of ourselves and not be too influenced by others. But they give even more importance to taking care of our spiritual side: they tell us that we are more than a body with a certain gender, age and role in society. We have a soul, and only by taking care of that part of us will we find meaning in our existence. As a result, we will naturally become happier and less preoccupied with the ups and downs of life.

We cannot love those we do not know. So, to love ourselves, we must first know ourselves well. Who am I if I am not my body, my job, my age? Who would I be if I were to lose everything in a shipwreck?

If I love myself, I will take care of my well-being, my health, my body, my professional life, my family, my social responsibilities, etc. But above all, I will take care of my essence—my core as a human being—and the well-being of my soul, the only thing that lasts when everything else is shaken.

In this sense, we can speak of the importance of taking care of our spiritual self-esteem. These are the moments of clarity in life when we review and reorder our hierarchy of values, prioritising our soul above everything else. This is the message that the great sages and masters bring us.

Introspection

Let us see how we can apply the advice of the sages to our lives by asking ourselves the following questions related to the four guidelines shared in this chapter:

1. Self-awareness, self-acceptance and leaving the rest in God's hands: *Am I aware of the relationship I have with myself? Do I treat myself as a good friend? Do I accept my weaknesses? How can I learn to focus only on what depends on me and leave the rest in God's or life's hands?*

2. Finding peace within ourselves: *Am I able to enjoy my solitude? On a scale of 0 to 10, how much value do I place on being at peace with myself? How could I have a better relationship with myself? Do I know and practise any techniques or exercises that brings me calm and tranquillity?*

3. Cultivating the values of a good person: *How do I evaluate myself based on the following values mentioned by the sages: tolerance, simplicity, existential joy, affection, faith, willpower, serenity, kindness and generosity? On which foot do I limp more and what values or human qualities could complete me as a person if I practised them more frequently?*

4. Taking care of our health and nutrition: *How does my health affect my self-esteem or self-perception? In my day-to-day life, am I more concerned about my health or my physical appearance? When I think about my diet, do I treat my body with respect and in the best possible way? Is there anything more I can do to lead a healthier life?*

My Notes:

THE SPIRITUAL PATH

If you train your mind well, let go of attachments and passions, and seek your inner light, you can attain inner freedom, Nirvana, even in this life.

—Buddha

Psychologist: *We are coming to the end of our coffee-meet. I believe we have learnt a lot about life, how to relate to others without losing our peace of mind, and how to deal better with conditions like anxiety and depression.*

But your messages certainly go beyond the mundane aspects of life, which is why I would like to delve a little deeper into the spiritual theme. I think this would help many of us explore our inner world further.

What characterises a spiritually advanced person, i.e., a yogi or a spiritual master?

Lao Tzu: We could mention many things. But some characteristics of a self-realised person are that they lead by example, and have no anxiety about winning or losing anything. They act without expecting rewards in return. And because they do not seek to take advantage of anyone or anything, people trust them.

Buddha: A spiritually wise person speaks little and lives by what he says. He is free from desires, expectations and hatred and maintains clarity of mind. Also, I would call a person who lives in contemplation and has attained inner enlightenment a liberated soul.

Krishna: I agree with Lao Tzu that this is a subject that deserves more time, but for now, I will add that the sage is one who acts without desire or expectation, is dependent on nothing and is grateful. But the yogi goes further because they have reached a state where they are able to see the light within and are one with God.

A YOGI ACTS WITHOUT EXPECTING ANYTHING IN RETURN, FREE FROM WORLDLY DESIRES AND ATTACHMENTS, SEEKING INNER ENLIGHTENMENT

Psychologist: *Many people only believe in what they are able to see or experience for themselves, and this makes them consider spirituality as 'naïve blind faith', as something that does not really exist. Can you share your thoughts on this topic?*

Lao Tzu: Look, when you think you already know everything, it is difficult to be guided by the wise. But when you accept that you know nothing, you find your way. Because not knowing is true wisdom, and to presume that you already know everything is a disease. You have to first realise that you are ill before you can be healed.

Krishna: What Lao Tzu says has to do with the fact that many people lack inner vision, and that is why they refer to the outer world and say, 'This is all there is.' To truly immerse ourselves in authentic yoga and see the truth within, we must be able to leave behind established theories and the existing literature.

Buddha: It is a pity, yes, because people who think that the truth is a lie and that the lie is a truth have the wrong mindset and they get lost on the incorrect path. To a person who does not believe in nirvana, I would say: find a devout person of noble spirit, a person with inner light who is not influenced by what happens in life. Follow this person for a while and see how it changes your life.

LEAVE YOUR PREJUDICES BEHIND, RECOGNISE THAT YOU KNOW NOTHING AND LOOK FOR A WISER PERSON FROM WHOM YOU CAN LEARN

Psychologist: *Is it fair to say that while some people are a little more open or sensitive to spirituality, there are more who have closed their minds to the concept and may never be interested in their soul? Is this how it is?*

Lao: That's right, and it all depends on our level of consciousness. Because when a conscious person hears about the Tao, they are immediately attracted to it. When a normal person hears about the Tao, they may swing between interest and doubt about the concept. When an ignorant person hears about the Tao, they laugh and make fun of it.

Buddha: The ignorant who has a closed mind despises the teachings of great souls and so harms himself.

Krishna: Unfortunately, those who have no faith do not take refuge in God and remain stuck in the cycle of life and death. Ignorant people continue to be stuck in darkness.

THE SPIRITUALLY IGNORANT HARM THEMSELVES; BE MORE AWARE AND NURTURE AN INTELLIGENT FAITH

Psychologist: *Krishna has commented on the cycle of life and death. Is it true that this life is not the first one we live, and that it may not be the last one either?*

Krishna: Of course. Just as a person goes through the phases of life—from childhood to old age—the soul also passes from one body to a new one. All of us have already gone through many lives. The enlightened person knows this truth.

Buddha: I have lived many lives, always hoping to meet the Creator. Now I have met him and I know that I will not return to this cycle of life and death. My mind has known nirvana. When you go beyond the illusion of samsara, you overcome, at last, the cycle of the transmigration of souls—one which is very difficult to escape. You cross to the other shore and merge with nirvana.

Lao Tzu: I would add that the Tao is always within us and is immortal.

THE SOUL IS IMMORTAL AND IS TOO ATTACHED TO THE MATERIAL—BE AWARE OF THIS TRUTH AND TRY TO FREE YOURSELF WITH SPIRITUAL PRACTICE

Psychologist: *If we start from the idea of reincarnation, is it possible to escape the almost-infinite cycle of life and death? Would it be possible for us if we began trying now, in this lifetime?*

Buddha: If you train your mind well, let go of attachments and passions and seek your inner light, you can attain inner freedom—nirvana—even in this life. The path of the reincarnating soul is both long and painful. We are tied to a strong chain that is very difficult to break. But it is possible.

Krishna: It is not easy to attain liberation, but it is certainly possible. Those who surrender their actions to God and worship him, and who practise concentration through yoga, will be liberated from the cycle of life and death.

Lao Tzu: When you realise your origin, you will know true wisdom. If you remain attuned to the Tao, your whole being will be in harmony. How do I know that what I say is true? Because I have seen it within myself.

WITH THE AID OF MEDITATIVE SPIRITUAL PRACTICE, YOU CAN ACHIEVE INNER FREEDOM IN THIS LIFE

Psychologist: *Thank you, I think we have managed to learn a little more about this complex subject. On a final note, can you share your thoughts on what a person aspiring to spirituality should do, and do you have any advice on how to start on the path of yoga?*

Buddha: The first thing I would say is that you have to make an effort; no one else will do it for you. The great souls of the past only show the way. Those who take the preachings of the sages seriously will find true freedom.

Krishna: Follow the path of yoga, for I assure you that on this journey, you will never take a false step and you need not be afraid of anything. Even a small step forward is already a valuable one. It takes a lot of determination, as Buddha says, and you must follow this path faithfully without expecting an immediate reward. When you can gather all your senses within yourself like the tortoise that withdraws into its shell, you will gain the inner vision.

Lao Tzu: Some say my teachings are absurd, and others say they are difficult to practise. I will tell you that if you look within yourself, you will find the meaning of my teachings. And if you put them into practice, they will elevate your inner self. If you want to know me, I will be waiting for you in your heart.

THIS IS A DIFFICULT PATH, BUT IT IS WORTH IT; TRY HARD, LOOK FOR THE RIGHT GUIDE, PRACTISE AND KEEP THE FAITH

The coffee-meet has come to an end. The four are still seated. The psychologist brings his hands together and says goodbye, grateful for the pearls of wisdom shared during the interview. Their cups are empty, but their hearts are full.

We hope that the reader ends this book in the same way, with the cup of their mind empty and prepared to be filled with the new things they learn, with a heart full of hope, love and wisdom.

Guidance from Krishna, Buddha and Lao Tzu

1#

A yogi acts without expecting anything in return, free from worldly desires and attachments, seeking inner enlightenment

2#

Leave your prejudices behind, recognise that you know nothing and look for a wiser person from whom you can learn

3#

The spiritually ignorant harm themselves; be more aware and nurture an intelligent faith

4#

The soul is immortal and is too attached to the material—be aware of this truth and try to free yourself with spiritual practice

5#

With the aid of meditative spiritual practice, you can achieve inner freedom in this life

6#

This is a difficult path, but it is worth it; try hard, look for the right guide, practise and keep the faith

The Psychologist Reflects

Krishna, Buddha and Lao Tzu have spoken to us about various important issues in life and have shared their advice with us throughout this book. We see that many of the problems we suffer from today are similar to problems that plagued people hundreds and thousands of years ago: the nature of the human mind remains the same.

However, the sages have repeated over and over again throughout human history the recipe for freedom from suffering and the path to true peace: discover our spirituality, realise our origin and identity beyond this body and mind, and work on our inner self.

Krishna, Buddha and Lao Tzu, as well as other sages and mystics in human history, agree on this. They warn us that no matter how much social power, popularity or wealth we achieve, we cannot find true happiness in the material world. Because the mind is never satisfied, and this essential problem can never be solved at the rational level alone, no matter how 'ideal' our life might seem.

Of course, the solution proposed to us is spiritual and is not easy; it is reserved only for those who are truly interested and willing to follow the spiritual path, investing their time and effort, and prepared to let go of their ego. Is there anything that can be achieved without the dedication of energy, attention and time?

Anyway, whether we are more or less interested in what they preach, we can still benefit from their philosophy, values and wisdom. They can always be our source of inspiration and personal development.

And if we visualise ourselves with sages by our side, accompanying us through our daily lives and helping us to face our problems, everything will surely work out for the best.

Introspection

Let us look at how we might take the first steps as a spiritual seeker. Krishna, Buddha and Lao Tzu have left us some guidelines for following this special path.

1. Acting without expecting anything in return, having fewer worldly desires and attachments: *In what ways am I aware of my desires and attachments, and how do they influence my well-being? Have I ever done something I thought was right without expecting anything in return? How did I feel? How do the results of my actions influence me?*

2. Recognising that we know next to nothing and looking for a suitable spiritual guide: *Am I open-minded about issues such as life, death, the soul and faith? How am I influenced by the ideas I have about these concepts? Am I willing to investigate what a spiritual guide is and how the spiritual disciple–teacher relationship works? How would I benefit from having a spiritual guide?*

3. Being open to spirituality and having faith: *What can I say about my faith? How important is faith in my life? Why do I think the wise insist so much on having faith? What hinders me and what helps me have more faith?*

4. Understanding how karma and reincarnation work: *How have I understood the subject of the cycle of life and death that the sages talk about in this book? How can I learn more about this subject? What practical use does the philosophy of reincarnation and karma have for me when it comes to being a better person in my day-to-day life?*

5. Tuning into our true essence and seeking inner freedom: *From what I understood from the answers, how does the practice of yoga, or spiritual meditation, relate to inner liberation (samadhi or nirvana)? How can I learn more about the true spiritual yoga that the sages talk about in this book?*

6. Having a genuine intention and making an effort in the right direction: *What concrete things am I willing to do to investigate further and start with some spiritual practice? Based on an understanding of the answers, how would a spiritual practice help and benefit me in terms of dealing with the issues discussed in this book (anxiety, depression, anger, etc. …)?*

My Notes:

NOTES

Part of our effort involved adapting the messages of the protagonists into a more modern and everyday language. We have paraphrased passages from the *Dhammapada* (Buddha), *Bhagavad Gita* (Krishna) and *Tao Te Ching* (Lao Tzu) for easy understanding and to give them a contemporary feel.

The reference corresponding to the answers provided by the sages are given in brackets. For example: (C3:22 – relevant excerpt can be found in Chapter 3, paragraph 22.)

SOCIAL LIFE

Buddha (C17:227), Lao Tzu (C56), Krishna (C2:33-35)
Buddha (C16:209), Krishna (C3:16, 17), Lao Tzu (C33)
Buddha (C25:366), Lao Tzu (C20, C33), Krishna (C4:22)
Krishna (C17:20), Lao Tzu (C8), Buddha (C8:100)
Buddha (C4:50), Lao Tzu (C33), Krishna (C12:4)
Krishna (C18:47), Lao Tzu (C8, C79), Buddha (C18:249)

WORK

Krishna (C6:17), Lao Tzu (C9), Buddha (C23:325)
Buddha (C14:186, 187), Lao Tzu (C16, C37), Krishna (C3:17, 18, 19)
Buddha (C5:75), Lao Tzu (C77, C13), Krishna (C2:48)
Buddha (C5:68, 69), Lao Tzu (C18), Krishna (C3:6)
Krishna (C3:4,5,7), Buddha (C19:259), Lao Tzu (C45)
Krishna (C2:47, C3:19), Lao Tzu (C23, C77), Buddha (C1:2, C15:204)

DEPRESSION

Lao Tzu (C44), Krishna (C5:21), Buddha (C15:204)
Buddha (C16:209, 210, 211), Krishna (C2:38), Lao Tzu (C64)
Buddha (C13:170, C25:367), Krishna (C2:16), Lao Tzu (C74)
Buddha (C3:42), Krishna (C16:20, 21), Lao Tzu (C74)
Lao Tzu (C39), Krishna (C4:39, 40), Buddha (C3:38, 39)
Lao Tzu (C37), Buddha (C226), Krishna (C6:19)
Lao Tzu (C74), Krishna (C2:38), Buddha (C11:147, 151)
Buddha (C13:170, C11:154, C6:89), Lao Tzu (C50), Krishna (C2:27, 30)

ANXIETY

Lao Tzu (C16, C55), Krishna (C4:20-22), Buddha (C3:39)
Lao Tzu (C31), Buddha (C1:6), Krishna (C3:43)
Buddha (C14:194, C11:156), Krishna (C2:66), Lao Tzu (C26)
Lao Tzu (C10), Krishna (C6:10), Buddha (C1:1, 2)
Lao Tzu (C26), Buddha (C1:7, 8), Krishna (C6:5)
Lao Tzu (C64), Buddha (C9:117, 121), Krishna (C3:5, 6, 7, 8)

ANGER MANAGEMENT

Krishna (C2:63), Buddha (C17:222), Lao Tzu (C10)
Krishna (C3:37, 38), Buddha (C17:221), Lao Tzu (C63)
Buddha (C1:3, 4, 5), Lao Tzu (C67), Krishna (C3:34)
Buddha (C4:50), Lao Tzu (C68), Krishna (C16:21, 22)
Lao Tzu (C55), Krishna (C18:50, 51), Buddha (C17:225)
Buddha (C17:226), Lao Tzu (C67), Krishna (C6:6)

SELF-ESTEEM

Buddha (C50), Lao Tzu (C30), Krishna (C4:22)

Krishna (C3:30), Buddha (C8:104, 105), Lao Tzu (C62)

Buddha (C23:320, 321, 322), Lao Tzu (C16), Krishna (C16:1, 2, 3)

Krishna (C17:8), Buddha (C15:204), Lao Tzu (C41, C50)

THE SPIRITUAL PATH

Lao Tzu (C2, C22), Buddha (C1:20, C26:386), Krishna (C4:19-22, C5:24)

Lao Tzu (C65, C71), Krishna (C2:42, C2:51, 52, 53)

Buddha (C22:318, C15:208)

Lao Tzu (C41), Buddha (C12:164), Krishna (C9:3, C9:12)

Krishna (C2:12, 13, 22), Buddha (C11:153, 154, C26:414), Lao Tzu (C4, C6)

Buddha (C6:89, C21:302, C24:346), Krishna (C12:6-9), Lao Tzu (C14, C32, C21)

Buddha (C20:276), Krishna (C2:40, 41, C2:47, 48, 49, C2:58), Lao Tzu (C67, C70)

BIBLIOGRAPHY

Lao Tzu (1978). *El Libro del Tao.* [*Tao Te Ching*]. Ediciones Alfaguara, S.A.

Buddha (1977). *Dhammapada.* Buenos Aires: Editorial Dédalo.

El Bhagavad Gita (1980). Barcelona: Vision Libros, S.L.

Bhagavad Gita (1985). Barcelona: Editorial Humanitas.

Bhagavad Gita (1978). Barcelona: Editorial Bruguera, S.A.

Singh, Maharaj Charan. 'Quote of the Day.' *Radha Saomi Satsang Beas*, www.rssb.org. Accessed 26 July 2023.